How to utilize your summers to create
impressive college applications

GET YOUR SUMMER STRATEGY! on.

JESSICA GIVENS

Get Your Summer Strategy On!
How to Utilize Your Summers to Create Impressive College Applications
Jessica Givens

All-in-One Academics, a DBA of
SJG Professional Communications, Inc.
1129 W Pierce
Houston, TX 77019

www.allinoneacademics.com

ISBN-10: 0-9845964-8-8
ISBN-13: 978-0-9845964-8-5

Printed in the United States of America

Cover Design: Pear Creative

First Edition: May 2011

Acknowledgements:

We only have the information that we've presented in this book because of the many students who have trusted us to guide them in their educational pursuits. Without the wonderful influence of our students' families, our days would want for richness and depth, and we would lack the ability to relate to so many different students with such varied interests and talents. That said, here's to Baby J, LAB, Master P, Hanky D, Cami P, Lyndsey, Emma, Austin, Drewbie, KinsMan, Dub K, Big C, E Money, and Blake. You know who you are.

Thank you, Rachelle, Michael, and Morgan, who support us in even the most hare-brained schemes.

Jill, you planted the seed, and I cannot thank you enough for the inspiration.

Finally and most importantly, Mom and Dad, without your sincere concern and diligent editing, this book would not exist. We are so lucky to have you as our guides and guardians.

Table of Contents

Introduction

My name is Jessica Givens, and I unwittingly took a direct path towards guiding students to embracing their educational futures. There have been twists and turns along the way, but some strange hand has pushed me in this direction for as long as I can remember. I truly understand the tendency to procrastinate and vegetate because I was there; I did it. However, today the world has changed, and college educations are simultaneously becoming indispensable and losing value. You need to have an education to get a job that will pay the bills, and you will ideally go to the best school you get into and pay *as little as possible*.

For the last thirteen years, I have advised others on their admissions decisions – picking their schools, editing their essays, proofing their résumés, and helping them fill out their applications. I didn't ever foresee myself in that role. I just got lucky. And, it turned out I had a knack for building confidence in others and inspiring them to strive for excellence.

How did I get here?

In 1999, I got a job working for a major test preparation company as an SAT instructor because I needed to earn extra money while I completed the requirements to apply to dental school. At that point, I could only see the black and white of my future career options, meaning I had reduced the entire universe to four possible paths: the health professions, the legal profession, the MBA corporate world, and academia. I didn't feel inspired by any of those careers, but I couldn't imagine there was anything else.

Then, amid a sea of standardized tests, I discovered the puzzling world of admissions – of college, law school, medical school, dental school, grad school, and business school – and I loved the riddle. I thrived on putting the pieces of a person's life together to display a certain image, to help him capitalize on his strengths. While the applicants themselves were terrified to sit down and take the plunge into starting their applications, I could look from an outsider's perspective to see their accomplishments, and I could also spot the gaps that needed to be plugged. My clients overcame low test scores by beefing up their résumés and perfecting their essays. With each acceptance letter that arrived in the mail, I felt unexpected exhilaration, and I couldn't get enough of it. I wanted to spread the word and give more people the chance to surprise themselves. That's how I started my admissions business in 2005, and ever since, I have assisted all kinds of clients, with all kinds of numbers, in applying to school. Now, it's time to share some of the wisdom I've accumulated along the way.

Why am I focusing on summer programs?

The college résumé is becoming more important with each passing year, as the trusty SAT and ACT are losing credibility as predictors of academic success. Many colleges are declining to see test scores and, instead, are focusing on the accomplishments of their applicants. They can tell more about a student's desire to contribute to a college campus and society as a whole by examining a list of his or her involvements than by looking at a few suspect numbers on a page.

Now, colleges like Harvard, Yale, Duke, and Stanford will always put stock in standardized test scores because they can, but there again, they won't take an applicant solely because of his numbers. In fact, Harvard rejects almost 50% of its valedictorians and perfect SAT score applicants. Why? Because eggheads are a dime a dozen, and they're looking for the well-rounded superstar, not the testing whiz.

So, with building a rock-solid résumé in mind, summer – a period of zero commitment and zero expectation – takes on a sparkly sheen as the golden opportunity to delve into personal and community interests. You can do anything; anything except fritter away three months of useful, transformative potential experiences. You can mix up your summers, doing service, learning work skills, and having a wonderful time.

I want to say before we go any further is that I know you need your rest during this season. I firmly believe that today's expectations of teenagers have gone haywire, but the fact remains that we can't really fight that system right now. What we have to do is strategize, so that you can balance normal teenage fun with responsible, character-building activities.

The earlier you start to take advantage of your summers, the more comprehensive and compelling your résumé will be, so start now. This is the first summer of the rest of your life! Even if you are going into your senior year of high school, it's time to seize the day. The activities you do in future summers will help you if you intend to transfer to a more prestigious college later in your educational career, and if you decide to attend a graduate program, these experiences will worm their way into future applications. There is no time like the present to get moving.

Note to Parents:

In many ways, the writing of this book is geared towards kids, in the hopes that they will take their own destinies into their hands. However, we know that, many times, kids need the push from their parents to actually get involved in anything. If you are a parent reading this book, it can help you guide your child on the road to résumé greatness, and it can assist you in unlocking your child's passions. Summer is the best time for kids to figure out what they might enjoy doing for long periods of time in their lives, and that may be a fabulous predictor for what they should choose for a major in college.

We encourage parents *and* students to read this book, because you can both come to an understanding of what's available in the way of summer options. Please note that this book is not comprehensive because there's no way for it to be; there are literally thousands of programs out there, and we just picked the programs that seemed interesting to us. From your own, personal frame of reference, you may determine that completely different topics suit your and your student's interests. Just be willing to Google for a little while because it's quite likely that what you're looking for exists.

You can also use our website as a free resource. You'll find a substantial list of summer programs there, along with other useful tips for preparing for college.

1

Taking Stock of
Where You Are Now

The First Step towards a Productive Summer

In this introductory chapter, we're going to give you an idea of what you should be doing this summer, based on what grade you'll be starting in the fall. You will want to keep the suggestions in this chapter in mind as you consider the many options available to you as a motivated high school student. Some of the terms may seem unfamiliar, but, not to worry, you'll get all of the definitions and more as the book progresses.

Before you get started on making solid, résumé-boosting summer plans, you should sit down and write out a list of your activities. Break them up with the following headings:

- Sports
- Clubs
- Community service
- Work
- Other important hobbies/activities

You may have trouble coming up with examples for any or all of them, but don't stress: there is time to improve your résumé. Most likely, one or more of the above areas will be weaker than the others, and you'll be struggling to find something to write down. Those are the holes we're going to attempt to plug.

Obviously, if you're finding this book after 8th grade, you have a lot of time to create a dreamy college résumé, but if you are finding if after 11th, you might feel like there isn't enough time left. It's always worth it to make the most of a summer, but let's work backwards and discuss what you should do during each summer, depending on how much time you have left.

You can modify any of the following suggestions. Just stay active. And try to make your summer choices meaningful, so they elevate you among future college students.

For Rising Seniors (this is your last summer):

- Pick a community service project and do at least **75** hours.
- Do some sort of educational program, even if it's something you coordinate for yourself through the local library.
- Fill out your college applications as soon as they are released (usually August 1).
- Finish any SAT/ACT preparation you feel you need. Definitely purchase practice test books, so you can be exposed to as many questions and sample problems as possible. You will want your last test dates to be the September ACT and October SAT, if possible.

For Rising Juniors (two summers to go):

- Pick a community service organization that you can follow for the next 18 months. Finish

100 hours of service by December of Junior year, and then another 100 hours by November of Senior year. *Do at least **50** hours this summer*. Track your hours online to make sure you get the President's Volunteer Service Award. We'll talk about service awards in Chapter 5.

- Think about what you'll eventually select for a major. This is the perfect summer **to start a business or find an internship**. Consider working at either your own project or a local business for 4 weeks. You'll continue this project in some capacity next summer, as well.

- Start thinking about your SAT and ACT. You may not be ready in the math department, but you should start working on your reading and vocabulary skills. If you go on Amazon and look up "SAT vocabulary novel," you'll see a host of different new and used options. These books integrate tough vocabulary into their stories and include definitions, so you can check if you understand the meaning in context. It may seem nerdy to read these books by the pool, but it makes tanning more productive.

- Visit your local colleges and get a feel for the campuses. Will you apply here? Do you have time to do a program here next summer?

For Rising Sophomores:

- Look into doing a mission trip. This is a great opportunity to build that part of your résumé profile because you really have more time on your hands than you will in future summers.
- Get started on the Congressional Award, if you haven't done so already. At the very least, complete the requirements for the Silver Certificate this summer. For more information, see Chapter 5.
- Consider doing a summer school program to a math or history credit out of the way. That will put you in a position to take more advanced classes later, which will look great on your transcript.
- Do as much service as possible this summer to make sure you'll be able to get the President's Volunteer Service Award this year.
- Look into doing an educational or sports program over the summer. Contact local museums, libraries, and universities to see what they're offering. You may not be old

enough to do a serious program, but every show of dedication will matter when you apply to college.

Rising Freshman (just finishing 8th grade):

- Pat yourself on the back for getting this book so early; you're going to have a memorable résumé by the end of high school!
- Get a jump start on community service. If you're diligent, you can four President's Volunteer Service Awards by the end of high school. See Chapter 5 for details on service awards.
- Register for the Congressional Award challenge, and lay out goals for yourself. You can get the Bronze Certificate this year and start working your way up. You should be able to at least get a Bronze Medal by the end of high school.
- Do an educational or artistic camp over the summer. Try to figure out what interests you – the arts, law, science, history, etc. – and let those interests guide you over the next three summers. By senior year, your application will look focused and convincing.
- Read!!! Whatever you can get your hands on, read it. There is no time like the present to

start building your vocabulary and improving your reading comprehension.

Keep in mind that there are always more options than we can ever possibly list in even the most insanely detailed handbook. Your job as you go forward is to take each of your activities seriously and weigh how it may affect the picture your résumé paints of you.

2

Lost Summer Syndrome
Filling the Void

Summer is a conflicted time. We have been programmed by society to see it as a season of ultimate relaxation: every day holds vast potential to slack off and forget the harsh realities of hard work. Let's face it, after winter break ends, you look forward to it every day, regardless of how many snow days or spring holidays you may get. It just feels like a birthright; you need and deserve that time off from thinking and being productive.

The truth is, you do deserve some relaxation during the summer. All semester long, you perform a delicate balancing act, artfully coordinating academics, extracurricular activities, and work. It's exhausting. But, do everything in moderation – even chilling out.

Your parents may let you off the hook because they know how hard you work during the school year, and they can't imagine how you do it all. Things have definitely changed since they were your age. They applied to college on a piece of paper. They probably took the SAT once, perhaps as a formality. There was no such thing as an AP class or a summer college preview program. They really could spend every day at the beach and face no consequence. Now, you really have to make the most of your time.

However, you need to take the initiative and continue the <u>fact and appearance</u> of commitment throughout the summer. You'll find that it's not so lame to get up a couple of hours earlier to volunteer or work at a place that inspires you, and many of your friends will have jobs or service placements, too. Those daytime commitments won't ruin your evenings; they'll just give you a purpose and add meaningful bullets to your college résumé.

As you know, it's harder and harder to get into the college of your choice, and colleges are looking for standout students, people who have gone above and beyond the call of duty. Summers are the ideal time to gain the experiences that create your unique image. They're really the only time of year when you can pick an activity or topic that interests you and pursue it to your heart's content. That's why you have to make the most of them. You don't necessarily have to get out of bed at 7:30 in the morning or sacrifice your weekends, but you can't just hang out with your friends from dawn until dusk... As a matter of fact, if you're smart, you can convince your friends to join in on your productive mission. Then, you don't have to suffer solo.

Here are 2 reasons why this is all so important:

1. Most colleges – except for the least competitive ones – want to know what you've done with your summers. They have an entire section reserved for you to discuss your summer activities, or they encourage you to include summer activities in your list of extracurricular commitments. Furthermore, admissions committees often like to see an expanded résumé that demonstrates

your involvement and dedication. On those résumés and extracurricular activity forms, missing summers stick out like sore thumbs. There's just no way around it.

On so many occasions, I have sat with seniors, helping them with their college applications, asking them, "What did you do before Junior year?" Each blank stare provides me with a clear answer. Nothing. What happened during that summer? No one can really remember. Maybe there was a family trip somewhere…maybe he worked at a movie theater…or was that when he watched seven seasons of "24" start to finish?

If you look back at your high school summers and feel a glazed look coming over your facial features, there is work to do. Until the summer before senior year, you can still make a change. Colleges want to see people who are improving with age, so if you haven't been active in the past, it's okay. What really matters is what you've done lately. It's time to put a positive spin on a slow start by making a change now.

2. Summer activities can really help add substance to your future college application. Through more intense involvement during summer, you'll figure out your specific likes and dislikes, a critical step in formulating career goals. Summer activities will also expose you to different issues - concepts you've never even heard of – and you'll be surprised by the new opinions you develop and unexpected goals you form. You will broaden your horizons and lay the groundwork to become a better you.

   For example, if you work at a hospital, you may wind up with a clearer picture of your thoughts on healthcare, or if you volunteer at a homeless shelter, you may have a redefined view on poverty. With a personal set of beliefs about a particular issue, you will find yourself developing a far greater chance of writing a compelling college admissions essay. You will be able to infuse passion into the words that fill the often stodgy essay format, rather than trying to guess what would sound good for the admissions committees to hear – that approach has been played out way too many times, and admissions officials can spot it a mile away.

You can also shape your goals through work or educational experience, and that will translate into a more focused, more impressive application, as well. With genuine ambitions and career interests, you will pick a totally different set of colleges for your application lists, ones that satisfy your educational needs, not just your party and social ones. That alone justifies the summer efforts, because you have no idea how much easier it will be for you to get a job if you have shown commitment all along in life. By taking this immediate step to make summers count, you will have laid the foundation to start off a winner.

What does the typical application look like?

The typical application has holes – lots of them. Like a piece of cheesecloth, the average application has spots of weakness, and you can see straight through them. You can do your best to patch and mend the less-than-special areas, but the fact is, many kids really do spend their summers doing nothing. That's why it's so easy to separate the motivated students from the slackers. Colleges can do it in a heartbeat.

A middle-of-the-road applicant has a B-average in school, a 23 on the ACT (1650 on the SAT), and a record of participating in one or two school activities, maybe working 20 hours a week at a retail job during the summer. This kid slept late and hung out with his friends, making the least of summer's seemingly endless time. There is nothing remarkable about this person, and he does not shine. This applicant may get into a low-to-middle end college, but definitely won't get scholarship money or be offered any stellar options.

Things could have been remarkably different for this applicant had she volunteered on a church mission trip for two weeks, or if she had gotten up two hours earlier and performed community service before heading off to work at the mall. With a certain amount of community service hours, she might have gotten a service award or two, and maybe would have been put in the running for local recognition. Unfortunately, her college application will have blank spots. It didn't have to be that way. Even with low numbers, this person could have had a healthy résumé that would show integrity and dedication.

As long as this person still has a three-month summer ahead of him or her, we can make meaningful change, and you'll be surprised at the transformation of this person's application and potential. The Lost Summer Syndrome does not have to be terminal; together, we can cure it! With some serious cooperation, a determined effort can still save an application from the great academic waste bin.

Let's get started!

3

Résumés

Build Up, Not Out

It can sometimes be tempting in high school to join twelve different clubs, do sixteen different service projects, and play a different sport each year. But at the end of four years, what does anybody know about your interests or passions? Very little.

Colleges want to see consistency and leadership in a few organizations. They want to know that you've challenged yourself to go above and beyond, revealing a strong motivation to succeed in the areas where you commit yourself.

That's why this chapter is so important: because you need to look at your résumé and see what trends it reflects. If you appear as a student who bounces from one activity to the next, then you may want to tone down the variety and hone in on a select few places where you can shine.

Remember, you can do anything you want. If you start a band, that's fantastic. In your résumé, you can talk about benefit shows you play for the community, competitions you've entered (both personally and with your band), and awards you've won. And if you aren't playing benefit shows for free yet, start doing it. We mentioned it earlier in the paragraph because it shows that you're doing more with your musical interests than pounding on guitars and drums in your parents' garage.

Again, colleges want to see your interests. They want to know who you're going to be on their college campus. Furthermore, your résumé lets them know what you've been doing in the afternoons. Show them you've been busy!

Doing an Evaluation

We're going to introduce you to Paulina and Janet, both of whom have B+ averages in school and test scores in the 80th percentile (1800 SAT; 25 ACT). Therefore, with respect to numbers, the two girls are really the same. Let's look for differences by analyzing their current résumés:

Paulina Smiley, a rising senior from Akron, Ohio:

Extracurricular activities:

Firestone High School Volleyball Team $(9^{th} - 11^{th})$
- 8 hrs/wk; 10 wks/yr
- Team member $(9^{th}, 10^{th})$
- JV Team Captain (11th)

Firestone High School Track Team $(9^{th} - 12^{th})$
- 6 hrs/wk; 8 wks/yr
- 100 meter dash

Firestone High School Cheerleading Team (12th)
- 12 hrs/wk; 8 wks/yr
- Varsity cheerleader
- Made spirit boxes for Varsity football players
- Painted signs for school

Investment Club $(9^{th} - 12^{th})$
- 2 hrs/wk; 18 wks/yr
- Club member $(9^{th} - 11^{th})$

- Treasurer (12th)
- Attended monthly meetings and events

Office Assistant   (11th)
- 4 hrs/wk; 36 wks/yr
- Junior Class Counselor's Office

Cooking Club   (9th)
- 3 hrs/wk; 8 wks/yr
- Member
- Attended events and helped with culinary festival

Spanish Club   (11th – 12th)
- 1 hr/wk; 6 wks/yr
- Member
- Practiced conversational skills and learned about Spanish culture

Community Service:

St. Martin's Episcopal Church Youth Group (9th – 12th)
- Worked on various projects with my church youth group
- Served Christmas dinner at Akron Food Bank
- Prepared gift baskets for children going through chemotherapy
- Led children's worship services
- 30 total hours of service

American Diabetes Association (9th)
- Served dinner at annual Halloween fundraiser
- 8 hours of service

Feed the Homeless (11th)
- - Made sandwiches for delivery to people living on the streets
- - 12 hours of service

Mission Trip to Amesuza, West Virginia   (10th)
- - Traveled with members of my church community to an impoverished community to rebuild homes
- - Successfully roofed, sided, and painted 14 homes over Spring Break
- - 90 total hours of service

Summer Activities:

Nellie's Volleyball Camp   (9th – 11th)
- - Two-week, sleepaway camp in New Ulm, Ohio
- - Practiced volleyball to prepare for the fall season

Edwards Cinema   (11th – 12th)
- - Worked as a cashier at a movie theater
- - Helped with concession sales and cleaned theaters after-hours

Janet Lopez, a rising senior from Midland, Texas:

Extracurricular Activities:

Environmental Awareness Club   ($10^{th} - 12^{th}$)
- Learned how to protect the environment
- Gave annual informative program for student body
- Planned first annual tree planting event at the district headquarters
- Secretary (10th)
- Vice President (11th)
- President (12th)

Astronomy Club   ($10^{th} - 12^{th}$)
- Learned how to use a telescope for amateur astronomy
- Took field trips with club members to the University of Texas Observatory to see larger astronomical events
- Founding member
- Social Chair (11th)

West Texas Astronomers   ($9^{th} - 12^{th}$)
- Club member
- Attend lectures and group meetings to study the stars
- Work at monthly "Star Parties," where people come to observe the changes in the night sky at the first Quarter Moon

Physics Club   ($11^{th} - 12^{th}$)
- Selected by Physics teacher on the basis of my Physics I grade to participate in this club

- Study Physics in the natural world
- Create a yearly Physics project. Last year, we built a car out of a shoe. This year, we will build a small rollercoaster.

Community Service:

Project Mentor $(10^{th} - 12^{th})$

- Tutored fourth and fifth grade students in science and math on a weekly basis throughout the school year
- Served as a role model for children in the program
- 4 hrs/wk, 30 wks/yr
- 270 hours of service to date

Project Mentor Summer Volunteer (9th)

- Worked at Midland Community Center with kids whose parents needed help with daycare during the summer
- Showed educational movies and helped kids learn about science in a fun way.
- 50 hours of service

Rio Grande Cleanup Effort (11th)

- Picked up trash along the banks of the Rio Grande
- Tested water for pollutants
- 25 hours of service

Summer Activities:

"Rio Grande" Summer Study Program   (11th)
- Through the UTEP Center for Archaeological Research
- Studied the natural and cultural landscapes along the Rio Grande
- Worked with archaeologists, historians, environmentalists, and biologists to learn the basics of scientific research
- A five-week program

Mathematics Research Training Camp   (10th)
- Selected to attend a math exploration program at Texas A&M University College Station, TX
- Learned about how to approach mathematical problems
- A four-week program

University of Texas Global Ethics and Conflict Resolution Symposium   (12th)
- Discussed environmental and social issues around the world
- Developed and researched solutions in small groups
- Presented our findings to the entire group
- A one-week program

Personal Research Project   (12th)
- "Tracing the radius of hydrocarbons around 21st century oil wells, compared with oil wells from the 1990s"
- Took soil samples at varying distances from the center of active oil wells

- Used facilities at the UT Permian Basin to determine the concentration of petroleum in the soil
- Will present my findings at the UT Permian Basin Science Competition
- A 10-week commitment

Looking at Paulina and Janet, side-by-side:

If you had to evaluate Paulina and Janet, what would you see? Both look like they're involved; both look hardworking. So, what separates them? It's time to inspect them under the magnifying glass.

What is Paulina's experience? She's in a bunch of sports and school clubs; she has diversified and joined a wide variety of clubs. She is clearly athletic; after all, she plays volleyball, runs track, and performs cheers for her school. In her sports, she has held leadership positions, as Captain of the volleyball team and as Varsity cheerleader. Next, Paulina has shown an interest in her community, by working with her church and spending her free time as a volunteer on mission projects. On that level, Paulina appears to be a responsible citizen who thinks about the comfort and happiness of others. Finally, Paulina has shown an interest in academics because she has spent her summer in an educational program at a nearby university. Yes, on the surface, Paulina looks pretty well rounded.

Let's do a superficial analysis of the résumé sections she's filled so far.

Whip out a pen and check the boxes:
- ☐ School involvement
- ☐ Community involvement
- ☐ Time management
- ☐ Academic dedication

You could really check each of these boxes without concern. That's because Paulina has met each of these criteria. You might wonder about the time management option, but in order to maintain good grades and participate in so many extracurricular activities, a person has to be able to balance time. Paulina has held leadership positions and kept good grades; therefore, it is reasonable to infer that Paulina possesses the ability to organize and manage her time effectively.

Yes, she has fulfilled the criteria that most universities value... but I still might not accept her to a competitive college. Or, at least, I wouldn't put her at the top of my list. Why not? Well, can you answer this question: What is Paulina's passion?

I can't.

Paulina has spread herself around so much that I can't really pinpoint what interests her. She clearly has school spirit and is involved in campus events, so that is attractive. I know that if she comes to my university, she will join organizations and, perhaps, take on leadership positions. However, I'm not sure that she is going to plow forward to success in any one area, and I don't have any clue what she might choose as a major. She participates in Investment Club during the school year, but she's done a science summer program – and she's only done one of those summer programs. Was she feeling out her interests, or did she join the science program merely to pad her résumé? I can't detect any meaningful pattern.

If I were to do a little detective work, I bet I would find out that someone told her, "Colleges like to see community service on your résumé." That's probably why she has spotty, small projects, rather than a long-term commitment. She joined all of those clubs for the same reason, most likely. That doesn't really bother me, though; it's almost universal on college applications.

Her summers are what really grate on my nerves. Where did they go? She had 10-12 weeks of summertime before 9th, 10th, and 11th grades... and all she did was one volleyball camp? That leaves at least 8 weeks unaccounted for each summer. The vast, empty space in Paulina's summers sticks out like a sore thumb because it says, regardless of her many commitments during the school year, that Paulina does not prioritize her time well. Students need to understand that seasoned admissions committees can spot those holes in a résumé. Admissions representatives want to see continuity throughout the year, and it would have been fine for Paulina to skip out on Cooking Club, but add a summer financial project to complement her school-time commitment to Investment Club.

Overall, Paulina comes away looking like a valuable addition to a less competitive university that is not overly concerned with the future goals of its students, but she's going to be hard-pressed to gain entry into a highly selective or honors program.

Now, let's look at **Janet**. What interests her? What makes her tick? It's pretty clear. Janet is a science and math nerd. Look at the clubs she has joined: Physics, Astronomy, and Environmental Awareness. Her community service involves her passion for science and math, and her summer experiences crystallize the picture of Janet as a future scientist.

Unlike Paulina, Janet has used her summers to delve deeper into her interests. She has studied on college campuses and worked with college professors to learn more about her educational path. Beginning in the summer between 9th and 10th grade, Janet has taken the initiative to make use of the free months of June, July, and August. I can tell where she's been and what she's done.

Please, note that Janet didn't do academics *all* summer. She only studied for 4-5 weeks until the most recent summer. That means she still had 6 weeks on her own to enjoy the break. However, she maximized her summer by reinforcing her commitment to science and math. Those summer programs gave her more intense experience than she possibly could have had during the school year, because of the many hours she could devote to learning. Furthermore, Janet will stand apart from her peers because so few kids actually seize their educational opportunities.

Janet does not have the volume that Paulina has, so her résumé has fewer bullet points. However, it's easy to identify her key interests and see that she is sincere. She has built her résumé from the ground up, and as she stands surveying the landscape from the top of her well-constructed foundation, she can see far and wide. The horizon is visible on all sides; she can plan with confidence.

On the other hand, Paulina has developed a broad base, but her foundation is shaky because she has no clear commitment. Paulina will take another few years to reach the heights of dedication that Janet already has demonstrated. Therefore, Janet will be accepted into the more serious academic institutions, while Paulina will receive acceptance letters to broader, less competitive programs.

4

Academic Application Boosters

College Summer Programs

Applicants who value education always look good to admissions committees. This isn't a secret. After all, they're applying to *college*. That's why it's imperative that you investigate ways to build your educational profile during the summers. Flesh out your application with evidence of your commitment to academic excellence and add value to yourself as a candidate.

The best (and easiest) way to do that is to apply for programs at local universities or at universities that really interest you. Here's why:

First, those programs connect you to the university in a way that no mere campus visit can. Professors at the university can speak on your behalf because they know you intimately.

Second, you get a genuine feel for what it would be like to study at that school. Who knows? You might be completely turned off! It would be great to figure that out *before* you actually enroll there.

Third, you show that you are thinking beyond the basics of high school. Universities have wacky summer opportunities. You might study the connection between Astrophysics, Shakespeare, and a double-fudge brownie. And, the crazy courses would be taught by actual professors or engaged graduate students, who could show you the limitless possibilities created by educational integration at a university.

Through such programs, you'll walk away inspired and energized about your collegiate future.

So, where do you start? Most universities offer summer educational programs for high school students. Competitiveness varies, as does cost. Highly selective colleges, like the Ivies, Stanford, and MIT, may require a certain GPA or class rank, while your state university may have more open admissions standards.

Additionally, many private universities charge thousands of dollars. For instance, Stanford charges a minimum of $7,195 for an eight-week summer program, plus a $75 application fee, but they often offer scholarships for good applicants with financial need. Public universities usually have many options, and those programs may even be **free**. If you qualify, you can go, and money won't stand in your way. Regardless, you will be able to find a program that meets your needs and fits your budget. It just may take a little research.

What's generally required to participate in summer programs at universities?

1. An official transcript from your school
2. Your current SAT or ACT scores
3. A letter of recommendation, sometimes two
4. A completed application
5. A record of extracurricular/community involvement
6. Perhaps an essay
7. An application fee
8. A scholarship or financial aid application, if you want financial assistance

Those requirements are absolutely not set in stone, and each program has different standards. You have to look at the specific programs that appeal to *you*. As we mentioned earlier, many programs offered by state universities are actually free of charge or extremely reasonable, so the application fee may not apply, and you may not have to file for financial aid. It all varies.

However, you have to understand that these programs are all competitive to some degree, so you should put effort into your application. That's also why you should apply to more than one. It would be better for you to have three from which to choose, rather than get rejected by the only one on your list.

Many programs are able to eliminate lazy students just by requiring a transcript. If you can assemble your documents, you are miles ahead of many of your peers.

Let's talk about what kinds of programs exist. First, we'll talk about general categories, then about subject matter. We've put examples for each one, so you can get an idea of what's out there. You can look into these particular programs in greater detail, or find others that suit you more appropriately. The examples come from all over the country because you can truly spend your summer studying *anywhere*.

Basic Categories of University Summer Programs for High School Students:

1. For Credit

Some college preview programs actually enroll students in courses for college credit. This may or may not sound appealing to you. After all, it is summer, and you want to have fun, not to mention the fact that you have no idea what to expect from a college summer school program – especially if this is your first one!

I would advise against doing a for-credit program on your first summer college program. You need to get your feet wet and see how you adjust to being away from home. Even in not-for-credit programs, you will have research to do and problems to solve, so you don't have to take the "For-Credit" plunge right away.

Example of a For-Credit program:

Stanford University –
"High School Summer College"

This is a very competitive program, and students start applying here in January. The earlier, the better, because Stanford is one of the hottest, most amazing tickets in the country, and you won't be the first person who wants to use this program as an entrée into the university. It is open to rising juniors and seniors.

What the program entails:
- Participants take college-level courses with college students and college professors

- Participants receive Stanford credit and a Stanford transcript, which may be used at other universities
- Students get real grades, and while the program provides one-on-one tutoring and support, there can be no doubt that only motivated, mature students need apply
- The program lasts a minimum of 8 weeks (10 weeks for students in Physics)
- Participants take a minimum of 8 hours (2-3 classes)

Cost:
- Varies, depending on the number of credit hours
- Minimum cost = $7,195

Scholarship:
- Eligible students can receive scholarship funding
- An additional application is required, but well worth the effort!

For more information, use this web address and click around:
http://summer.stanford.edu/programs/program/high-school-summer-college-16-17-years-of-age

2. Not for credit

Most programs do not offer college credit to high school students. Instead, they serve as previews into the possibilities of college. These programs sometimes tend to be a little less competitive, but they can still be very prestigious. Not-for-credit programs allow students to relax and enjoy the experience of the college campus, as well as have a good time studying fun subject matter.

Many not-for-credit programs allow students to create their own projects, which the students present at the end of the program, both to parents and teachers. These programs introduce students to possible careers and give them the knowledge to plan a path to success.

Example of a Not-for-Credit program:

University of Miami – "Summer Studies in Architecture for High School Students"

This program will introduce high school kids (anywhere from $9^{th} - 12^{th}$ grades) to the concepts of environmental design. For students who are interested in drawing and architecture, it's wise to construct a portfolio over the summers, and the easiest way to jumpstart that daunting task is to join a program like this one.

While there are no grades given in this program, students do design work on their own projects and receive critiques from faculty and other professionals.

What the program entails:
- Participants work on three skill areas:
  - Environmental Awareness
  - Intellectual Development
  - Career Determination
- The program lasts three weeks, running Monday to Friday, from 9:30 AM to 12:00 noon
- Participants do not live on campus, so the program may be best for Miami natives
- The program is open to anyone interested in a career in architecture
- No need to send a transcript, test score, or letter of recommendation

Cost:
- $750

Scholarship:
-    Not available.

For more information, use this web address
and click around:
http://arc.miami.edu/programs/high-school-
summer/summer-studies-in-architecture

3. Free Programs to Qualified Candidates

Some universities offer free summer
opportunities for enrichment, understanding
that the financial burden of most summer
programs eliminates all but the wealthiest
applicants. These programs generally are
targeted towards minority students, including
racial minorities and women. You have to
Google free summer high school programs for
minorities to get a decent list, and even then,
you'll probably have to plow through a bunch
of garbage to get to the good stuff. However,
it's worth the effort because these programs
are plentiful and just as prestigious as any
paid program, sometimes even more so.
What's important to note, though, is that you
need to get these applications in early
because they are definitely competitive –

who doesn't want a free pre-college program?

Example of a Free Program:

*Indiana University –
Young Women's Institute*

Although women have made incredible strides in the working world over the last 50 years, they still haven't caught up in the business world. Many women feel that the business world prefers men, so they stay away from pursuing a career in that field. By exposing talented young women to the boundless possibilities of the business world, this program aims to change that sort of negative self-perception.

Funded by the Kelley School of Business and the John Deere Company, the Young Women's Institute gives participants an introduction to multiple aspects of business: Marketing, Entrepreneurship, Accounting, to name a few. Participants meet other motivated young women, which inspires both motivation and confidence.

What the program entails:

- Six nights and seven days of lectures and events to groom future businesswomen
- Participants learn to express their own strengths through personality sessions
- As they live together in university dorms, the girls join up in teams and complete one business project
- The program also teaches students and their parents about admissions into business programs around the country to help participants make the important transition from summer program to college major

- Cost: FREE

    o Cost includes all meals, housing, classes, etc.
    o Students just need to pay their way to Bloomington, IN

For more information, use this web address and click around:
http://kelley.iu.edu/ugrad/precollege/ywi.cfm

4. Residential Programs

In residential programs, students stay on campus throughout the duration of the program. Students meet a completely new group of friends and learn to share a room with a new friend, as well. Residential programs can be a little intimidating, but they are often extremely rewarding.

In residential programs, students tend to accomplish a great deal because they focus on their projects and bond with other participants.

Example of a Residential Program:

University of Kansas –
"Kansas Journalism Institute"

Some of us were born to write, and there is no doubt about it: even though newspapers and magazines are drying up on paper, global readers still crave the news. This program helps students who would like to consider a career in journalism, or who have an interest in yearbook or newspaper at school. The program has run for the last 48 years and commands respect in the field of journalism.

In this program, students do not receive credit, but they may choose from a wide variety of courses in the field of journalism, ranging from "News Magazine and Newspaper Design Fundamentals" to "Digital Photojournalism" to "Digital Media: Video and Audio Production."

What the program entails:
- Four nights and five days of immersion in journalism
- Morning and afternoon classes, followed by small group meetings to work on projects
- An awards ceremony at the end
- Students expected to stay on campus because of the program's collaborative environment

Cost:
- $425

Scholarship:
- Limited number of awards in the amount of $375
- In addition to the KJI registration form and $50 deposit, students must submit:

- o A scholarship application form
- o A letter of recommendation from a journalism or English teacher
- o A short personal statement, explaining your motivation, focus, and goals

For more information, use this web address and click around:
http://ehub.journalism.ku.edu/kji/

5. Commuter Programs

Most programs offer a commuter option for students who live nearby. This choice can definitely save money for participants, and it's a good way to start out in a college program. The only drawback of the commuter option is that you might miss out on some of the nighttime gossip and chit-chat, but in reality, you'll be at home, hanging out with your normal friends anyway!

Example of a Commuter-Only Program:

Drexel University –
"Music Industry Summer Program"

So, you're interested in music from a technical or business standpoint. That sort of information just isn't taught in the typical classroom. This is an intensive, week-long program that looks at the music industry as a whole. Students can take classes in songwriting, publishing, sound engineering, etc. While the course only lasts one week and students live off-campus, the course is jam-packed, and students will walk away with a world of new knowledge to apply to their future choices.

The program welcomes students who are at least 16 years old and are rising juniors or seniors. Applications are reviewed on a rolling basis, so you'll be considered as soon as you apply. If you are not accepted into the program, you will get your deposit back.

What the program entails:
- Students enroll in three courses
- Students attend class Monday through Friday, from 9:30 AM to 4:40 PM, breaking only for a one-hour lunch, which is provided by the program

- Students learn from industry professionals
- Students study in the university's recording labs, recording studios, and piano labs
- The program concludes with a reception that presents lectures by industry professionals and showcases musical talent from within the summer program

Cost:
- $1,300

Scholarship:
- Not available

For more information, use the following web address and click around:
http://www.drexel.edu/undergrad/summer/#music

6. **Longer programs (more than 3 weeks):**
   Some programs are a little intimidating because they require a student to commit to multiple weeks on campus; however, long programs can be great for students who are entering their junior or senior year and want to show dedication. Longer programs often allow students enough time to complete a

solid project, so this situation can be ideal for anyone who wants to enter a competition during the school year.

Example of a Longer Program:

The University of Chicago –
"Stones and Bones: A Practicum in
Paleontology"

While the University of Chicago offers a wide range of courses for high school students over the summer, this is an incredible program for students who are interested in fossils or natural history. Although it's easy to forget, not everyone wants to pursue a career in business, engineering, medicine, etc., and we *need* paleontologists in this world! Furthermore, the study of fossils lends itself to a career in geology, as well, which is an excellent building block for a future in the energy industry. So, if you have an interest in fossils, rocks, or history, this might be an excellent summer option, although it definitely is not cheap.

"Stones and Bones" begins in mid-June and runs until mid-July. It starts out in Chicago, where students take basic classes in paleontology, so that they don't enter the field completely ignorant of the goals and practices. After a week of classes at the University of Chicago, students travel to Wyoming for two weeks, where they work on an active archaeological dig. While in Wyoming, the participants camp and hike, carrying their provisions in backpacks and living right alongside the paleontologists. Then, the students return to the University of Chicago to learn about the Field Museum and the laboratory research conducted behind the scenes there.

The program is open to all high school students, from 14-18. Students <u>must</u> live on campus throughout the duration of the program. Students receive credit for 2 college classes upon completion of the program.

What the program entails:
- A four-week intensive exposure to paleontology

- Learning both in the classroom at University of Chicago and in the field at the Green River Formation in Wyoming
- The opportunity to see how museums preserve, catalog, and study their findings
- A combination of outdoor activity and classroom learning
- Students have to buy their plane tickets to Chicago, but travel to Wyoming is included in tuition

Cost:
- Tuition: $6,150
- Housing and transportation: $2,995
- Residential Program Fee: $280
- Student Life Fee: $310
- Student Health Insurance (optional): $822
- GRAND TOTAL: $10,557

Scholarship:
- Not mentioned

For more information, use this web address and click around:
https://summer.uchicago.edu/stones-and-bones.cfm

7. **Shorter Programs (Less than 3 weeks, sometimes as little as 1 day):**

Shorter programs are very targeted and very specific. They are not as much about giving exposure to college realities as they are about giving students information on one topic. These can be excellent introductions to career opportunities, and all students should participate in a few of these programs.

Short programs tend to be quite affordable, and they are very worthwhile because they show commitment, but still allow students to maintain summer jobs and other commitments.

Example of a Shorter Program:

The University of Maine –
"Consider Engineering Summer Program"

Many programs introduce students to the profession of engineering. This one stands out because of the fact that it is free to participants. Students join in nearly 20 activities, working under the watchful eye of multiple UMaine faculty, professional engineers, and engineering students.

Acceptance is competitive, with only 2/3 of applicants invited to attend. Participants need to be rising seniors, who have completed *at least 3 years of math and science*.

There are three sets of program dates, all of which occur during July.

What the program entails:
- A four-day camp experience
- Students live in residence halls at the University of Maine
- Participants learn how engineering differs from a career in pure science

Cost:
FREE!!!

Scholarship:
Not necessary.

For more information, use the following web address and click around:
http://www.mainepulpaper.org/considerengineering/considere ngineering.htm

Within those very general categories listed, you need to look for programs that actually interest you. There are more options than you can imagine, so if you are into film, literature, medicine, etc., your interests *can* be accommodated. It just might take some searching.

SUBJECT-SPECIFIC SUMMER PROGRAMS

Here are some general areas of focus that people often find interesting and some sample programs you might check out for each, but with less description than we used above:

Science

- *University of Michigan – "Michigan Math and Science Scholars 2011"*
  - **How long?** Two-week sessions
  - **What?** Students take one course, such as Fibonacci Numbers and Roller Coaster Physics
  - **Who?** Open to all students who have completed at least one year of high school
  - **Where?** Commuter or Residential Program on the Ann Arbor campus
  - **How much?** Commuter: $1,000. Residential: $1,700.
  - **Financial aid?** Available.
  - **Link?** http://www.math.lsa.umich.edu/mmss/index.html

Engineering

- *The University of Notre Dame – "Introduction to Engineering"*
  - **How long?** 2 weeks

- **What?**   A smorgasbord of information about careers in engineering and the educational path to get there
- **Who?**   Rising seniors
- **Where?**   The Notre Dame campus in South Bend, Indiana
- **How much?** $1,750
- **Financial aid?**   Some partial scholarships available
- Link?   http://www.nd.edu/~iep/costs.html

Math

- *University of Utah – "Summer Mathematics Program for High School Students"*
    - **How long?**   3 weeks
    - **What?**   Study of "Explorations in Number Theory," cryptography, an introduction to Python language, and the study of mathematical applications
    - **Who?**   Preferably rising seniors, must have completed pre-calculus
    - **Where?**   At the University of Utah in Salt Lake City; Primarily for commuters, but can be residential at an additional cost
    - **How much?**   Free to US citizens, nationals, and permanent residents
    - **Financial aid?**   Not necessary
    - **Link?** http://www.math.utah.edu/hsp/index.html

Writing

- *Sarah Lawrence College – "Summer Writer's Workshop for High School Students"*
  - **How long?** 5 days, 9 AM – 5 PM
  - **What?** Writing and theater workshops with a maximum of 15 participants per workshop, as well as individual meetings with workshop leaders
  - **Who?** All students entering 10th, 11th, and 12th grades
  - **Where?** Commuter program at Sarah Lawrence campus in Bronxville, NY
  - **How much?** $500
  - **Financial aid?** Partial scholarships available
  - **Link?**
    http://www.slc.edu/ce/pre-college/summer/index.html

Technology

- *Missouri University of Science and Technology – "EcoCAR Summer Camp"*
  - **How long?** 5 days
  - **What?** A program dedicated to Plug-in Hydrogen Eco-CARs, focusing on labs, modeling, and design contests
  - **Who?** 25 students entering 10th, 11th, and 12th grades, must attend a science high school that is a member of the National Consortium for Specialized Secondary Schools of Math, Science, and Technology

- **Where?** Residential program on the Missouri S&T campus in Rolla, Missouri
- **How much?** $750
- **Financial aid?** Not available
- **Link?**
  http://futurestudents.mst.edu/precollege/ecocar.html

Social Science

- *Illinois Institute of Technology – "Psychology Summer Program"*

  - **How long?** 5 days
  - What? An introduction to the field of psychology, helping students see psychological principles at work in everyday life
  - **Who?** All students entering 10th, 11th, and 12th grades
  - **Where?** Commuter program at Illinois Institute of Technology in Chicago, IL
  - **How much?** $485
  - **Financial aid?** Scholarships available
  - **Link?**
    http://www.iit.edu/undergrad_admission/psychology_summer.htm

As we mentioned before, the programs here represent only a sprinkling of what's available. You are going to have to do some searching on your own to find programs that meet your needs exactly.

So, how do you search for these programs?

First, we recommend using Google and searching for "high school," "program," and the name of whichever university interests you. You will get zillions of results, and you'll have to read through them.

Second, you'll need to call the university in question and make sure that you have all of the information. You need to know if they are still accepting applications and if the website has been updated. Also, those websites are sometimes a little tricky, and you might not see the link to the program that fits you. Don't give up before making a phone call.

So, out of the hundreds of phone numbers on the website, which one should you call? You should probably start with the office of undergraduate admissions. It definitely could happen that you wind up with a student answering the phone who doesn't know anything, so it's worthwhile to ask to speak to an admissions representative.

Here's a **suggested script** for your phone call:

"Good morning. My name is _____, and I was wondering what sort of program __(Insert name of university/college)___ offers for high school students over the summer."

There are two possible outcomes:

- If they know what you're talking about, they'll probably offer to email or mail you a copy of the brochure and application. It's as simple as that.

- If they don't, you should ask to speak to an admissions representative for your area.

This will set you on the path to finding the program for you. If they don't have a program that suits your needs, it's likely that they will know about options at another university. Remember, this is a process.

5

Raking in the Hours

Community Service over the Summer

There was a time when very few of us really did community service in high school. I personally volunteered at the Humane Horse Ranch in Houston, cleaning horse stalls and feeding retired racehorses. I probably only volunteered a total of 12 hours, and I could hold my head up high on a college application. Most of my competition had zero hours. However, that was 17 years ago. Things have changed. Not only do you need to be academically impressive, but you need to have a streak of Mother Teresa running through your veins, as well. Unfortunately, though, not all community service is created equal... you need to be judicious in the service hours you pick up and try to be consistent in the organizations you choose.

In the summer, you can get a ton of hours to qualify for service awards and set a strong pace for the fall. However, those hours need to qualify!!! Not to mention the fact that they should look good on paper. You need to look like you gave up meaningful time.

GOING ABROAD
Glamour service versus genuine altruism

Community service should not feel like a luxury vacation. If you're staying in a posh Monterrey hotel while you volunteer with the poor communities of Mexico, then you're not exactly learning to appreciate the suffering that those people are enduring. And, if you are traveling all the way to Guatemala for three weeks, but only completing 12 hours of service in-between your zipline tours of the jungle, then you aren't really doing the world a favor. You want your service to look like you care, enough to sacrifice some of the comforts to give back and make a genuine difference.

That means you need to be discerning when you pick a program. You don't have to leave the United States, that's for sure. But, if you decide to go abroad, then you should choose a program that has several important characteristics:

STIPULATION #1
The program is part of an established organization
in the area

It's best to work with a program that has its roots firmly planted in an area, because those projects make progress and have real placements for their volunteers. This means that there should be some program in place that runs year-round, regardless of the volunteers that come in and out.

The long-term existence of the organization matters for a couple of reasons. First, it's more likely to have a relationship with the community. Such organizations are well-respected and often protected by the community. The members of the community trust what the organization offers, and volunteers are welcomed with open arms. Second, volunteers don't have to waste time figuring out what to do with their time. The organization has needs that volunteers fill, and they know where to assign particular types of people. High school students may wind up teaching English or helping with crafts, and while adults could find themselves in the kitchen or working with the elderly or sick. Anyone could wind up on a project build. However, building projects with established organizations are likely to be more orderly and better planned. The directors of the year-round staff know what needs to be accomplished, and they put volunteers to work in meaningful tasks.

It also helps that established organizations are verifiable, and colleges can Google them to see what participants really do.

STIPULATION #2

The program spends the majority of time on a service project.

While it is very cool to go abroad and check out beaches and mountains, it can be a real waste of time (from a résumé-building perspective) to spend three weeks being just as unproductive as you would be at home. If you are hanging out and getting a tan, you might as well have just gone on vacation.

Service should not be a secondary component of the trip; it should be the primary focus. Some trips abroad focus more on getting three hours of college credit than on doing service. It's harder to sell the getting-credit-out-of-the-way motive to colleges than it is to warm their hearts by showing sincere concern for your fellow human.

Let's talk about two programs, both of which are valuable, but which need to used differently on college applications.

Name of Program	Belize Dolphin Studies
Brought to you by	Academic Treks
Focus of trip	Scuba diving and snorkeling to explore reefs and study dolphin habitats, biology, and behavior

Service hours	12+
Length of trip	21 days
Tuition	$5,580
College credit	3 natural science credits from Lesley University
Link	http://www.academictreks.com/

Name of Program	Conservation in Costa Rica
Brought to you by	Projects Abroad
Focus of trip	Working on a conservation project at Barra Honda National park, teaching children in Liberia, and taking optional Spanish classes
Service hours	80
Length of trip	14
Tuition	$2,895
College credit	None
Link	www.projects-abroad.org

Both of those programs are extremely cool, and I have had students do both. It just depends on their situation.

For students who have an interest in pursuing a career in Marine Biology, it's probably a better idea to do the Academic Treks program. In that case, an applicant can write an informed admissions essay and target his or her college application to demonstrate well-considered interest. The Academic Treks program will build a marine-focused résumé up, but it might build a generic résumé out.

Another reason students and parents might choose the Academic Treks program is that it offers more planned activities for enjoying the geography and wildlife of Belize. It's almost like camp, but abroad. If I have a student who is hard to convince about doing a summer program, I will encourage him or her to go this slightly more glamorous route. It still looks better than laying out or lifeguarding all summer.

Still, it bothers me that in 3 weeks, students only earn 12 hours of service (although they could get more hours, depending on their choices while there – they could always go above and beyond). If you're going to travel all the way to Belize, it seems like you should do more service than that!!!

That's why I prefer the Projects Abroad program for the general applicant. The Projects Abroad program is committed to service, not to one specific area of interest, but to a community as a whole. A high school student could walk away with a completely different view of the United States after seeing street life in Liberia, Costa Rica.

That firsthand exposure would give a student more to write about in an admissions essay. Additionally, the large number of hours would help that student be competitive in scholarship applications that ask about service commitments and in receiving service-based awards. Summer is probably the only time of year when a student can get 120 hours in a big chunk, and it's worth the small sacrifice of summer sluggishness to add such remarkable value to your college applications!

STIPULATION #3

The program immerses participants in the culture.

It's best if students actually stay in the midst of their service project, in volunteer housing. When participants are sheltered from reality by staying in a nice hotel near the volunteer site, they lose touch with the depth of suffering that goes on outside the bubble of our everyday lives.

Colleges groom their students not only to be successful contributors to society through work but also to become compassionate leaders. Colleges themselves often sponsor service projects and fund their professors and students in community endeavors... This altruistic spirit gets very good press and improves a school's image, so it's an integral part of a college's overall plan for self-betterment.

By appreciating the value of service and reaching out to touch the lives of the less-fortunate, applicants demonstrate to admissions committees that, if accepted, they will help the college further its mission to change the world (and enhance its own reputation). That's a good thing to convey on an application!! That's why meaningful service MUST play a role on a student's application.

MISSION TRIPS

Incredible opportunities to give back, get a zillion hours of service, and have a blast.

Mission trips are generally organized by churches, mosques, or synagogues, so they often entail a religious component; however, that is not usually the main reason for the trip. Religious organizations often encourage kids to share with their neighbors and to give back to the least fortunate members of the population. Mission trips are often led by church officials or active members, and they don't generally involve any student fun time. They're all about work and good intentions, both positive indications on a college application.

Mission trips often give students over a hundred hours of community service, so with just one mission trip, a student can qualify for service awards and recognition. They are also quite inexpensive, so there is tremendous bang for your buck.

There is one way to make a mission trip look even better: to obtain a leadership position with the trip. If a student can become a project leader or a devotional leader, that makes the experience even more significant.

Most college applications give applicants the opportunity to fill in positions in each organization or activity listed. Rather than say "participant," it looks far better if a student is able to say, "Paint Crew Leader," or something similar. The more meat an application has, the better it looks, and the more involved a student is in his or her activities, the more those activities mean.

COMING UP WITH YOUR OWN THING

The best way for a student to show leadership and commitment to service is to take the bull by the horns and start his or her own service organization. It's not that hard... seriously! He or she can enlist friends to help in the effort, and all of a sudden, you are the founder of a brand-new community organization.

I know, this may sound overwhelming, but it may actually be easier – and definitely will be cheaper – than joining another organization on a trip. All you need is a little organization and a summer's-worth of free time. The cool thing is, with a unique, home-grown group, the service doesn't have to stop when the school year comes around; it can evolve into a year-round activity that feels good to do.

Let me give a run-down on the steps to start a grassroots service group. First, I'm going to list some basic steps for you to follow, and then, I am going to give a fleshed-out example.

1. Pick a group in need.
2. Think of something that group might need.
3. Call up four friends and ask them if they would want to get some community service hours.
4. Contact an organization that works with that group.
5. Ask that organization if it would mind letting people know about your new service.
6. Dedicate eight hours per week to the project: an organizational meeting on Monday and two hours of service a day, Tuesday, Wednesday, and Thursday. (obviously, the schedule would change during a school year)
7. Place a call or write an email to a local paper, so that they can write an article about your organization

Okay, so let's see this in action. The following story is something you could do.

My student, John, is going to start an organization to help the elderly in the City of Houston. He knows that elderly people would have a hard time doing work around their houses, and he wants to help with small tasks that they might have to pay someone to do, such as going to the grocery store or mowing the lawn. John is going to call the organization, "Able Bodies with Helping Hands" (ABHH).

He and his friends will contact three churches in the neighborhood to tell them about their plan, and the churches will post fliers to tell their members about the project. Because churches want to spread the word about service, all of the churches will make announcements to let community members know about ABHH, and within a week, John and his friends will have more than enough work to keep them busy.

ABHH is going to do basic chores for the people they help. Because the boys are young and resilient, they can do all sorts of helpful tasks, from cleaning out refrigerators to washing cars to painting front doors. None of these chores will change the world or cure cancer, but they are extremely helpful to those in need. We get so bogged down with the idea of making enormous change that we forget that, on a local level, people have great need of the smallest assistance.

John will let the community newspapers know about his work, and every paper wants to write about caring high school students, a dying breed that needs preservation. He can continue the work on weekends during the school year – maybe two Saturdays a month.

In the end, John will earn 175 service hours over the course of the year, qualify for the Silver President's Volunteer Service Award, and receive an honor at the Houston Livestock Show and Rodeo. His grades in school still look a little unimpressive, but he's got other things going for him on a résumé. He's going to get into a good college.

There are countless opportunities like this! It just takes some effort.

SERVE.GOV
A National Resource for Aspiring Volunteers

Even with all of our suggestions, you might find it hard to get started, so there are resources to help you make headway. In a contracting economy, the government is looking to volunteers to help out with its community programs, and it's doing so through **United We Serve,** at www.serve.gov.

Volunteers need a way to connect with programs and with each other, and so the Obama administration has put together an initiative to facilitate those connections. While the site allows volunteers to find local projects, what's really cool is that it provides thorough **volunteer toolkits**, which guide young volunteers through the entire process of putting a homegrown project together.

There are many lame websites volunteers out there, but *this is not one of them!!!* The site even advises you of how to contact local media, how to write a press release, and how to blast your message on the radio to recruit volunteers. You can post your project on the Serve.gov site, as well, and let the entire nation know what you are doing.

If you stick with a project that you find or create through the help of United We Serve, you will definitely have the potential to get some cool service awards that will glow on your college application.

THE PRESIDENT'S VOLUNTEER SERVICE AWARD:

The United States government recognizes people who put in an exceptional number of community service hours by granting four different levels of service awards: Bronze, Silver, Gold, and Congressional.

As young adults, you have to meet certain standards to qualify for the awards.

Bronze Level: 100-174 hours in one calendar year

Silver Level: 175-249 hours in one calendar year

Gold Level: 250+ hours in one calendar year

Your hours must be completed with a **Certifying Organization**, but almost any nonprofit or charity can become a certifying organization. The officials at the organization just need to go online and fill out the right forms.

*Talk to people at the organization where you're volunteering and ask them to go to: www.presidentialserviceawards.gov and click on **Become a Certifying Organization**.*

You will want to create a **Record of Service** to keep track of the amount of service you've completed over the course of a year. You can keep track of your hours on the award website.

It's important to note that a calendar year can begin and end whenever you want. It would probably be best for yours to begin June 1 and end May 31. That way you get the full summer to volunteer, and each school year can bring you a new award.

THE CONGRESSIONAL SERVICE AWARD:

This is a super-cool award because it's additive, which means you can start accumulating hours when you are 13.5 years old (yes, 13 and a half), and when you reach milestones, you can get new awards. What are we talking about?

It works like this: Congressional Awards come in two basic forms, **certificates** and **medals**. You can get a bronze, silver, or gold certificate, and you can get a bronze, silver, or gold medal. Medals require more hours than certificates.

Unlike the President's award, which is based only on service, the Congressional Award has four different components:

1. Volunteer Public Service – community service hours

2. Personal Development – something you do to improve yourself, like learning to play the piano or meeting goals towards becoming fluent in a new language

3. Physical Fitness – push yourself to go to the next level in a physical activity, like training for a half-marathon or improving your batting average in baseball

4. Expedition/Exploration – the most unusual part – participants must immerse themselves in an unfamiliar environment. Many kids choose to do campouts or wilderness treks, but some students immerse themselves in foreign cultures. A lot of kids team up with Congressional Award partners to accomplish this part of the challenge.

Important Note:

To qualify for the Congressional Award, you'll need an **adult sponsor**, who will help you set goals and verify that you've met your challenges. That sponsor can be anyone except a parent, relative, or friend.

We've had kids go all the way through the Congressional Award levels, to wind up with the Congressional Gold Medal by the time they graduate from high school. They can list that on applications for the rest of their lives –

remember, for many people, college is just the beginning – there's grad school, law school, med school. You can cash in on these personal development and service awards on each of those applications.

Since the Congressional Award process is a little tricky, you should really go online and look at it:

www.congressionalaward.org

Again, these are not the only awards available to committed, community-minded people. You should Google what's available locally and keep your eyes and ears open. You never know what's going to pop up. And, you might as well apply for any award you see. The worst thing that happens is you don't get it.

6

Showing Serious Intellectual Commitment

Summer Research Programs

When you think about research, you probably imagine scientists in white coats, tucked away in a laboratory, way more professional than you consider yourself. Here's the deal: Students all over the country are starting to do research in high school. Why? Because they can, and it looks good.

Some people think research sounds boring, and parts of it definitely are, but universities value research highly. Lots of their funding has to do with their research programs, and national recognition hinges upon a university's ability to show itself as a frontrunner in the discovery of knowledge. And, they expect their students to get in there and do research during college.

One interesting thing about doing research is that you can often get paid to do it. You might make as much as you would having a regular summer job, so there's no reason NOT to apply. You just have to seek out the ones that have what's called a "stipend." A stipend is another word for salary, but it's given to students in exchange for some sort of work.

A stipend is not taxed, so when it says that you make $1,300, it means that you really get a paycheck in that amount. When you work at a movie theater, you have to make about $1,700 to walk away with that total. If you need to make money over the summer, you should try to do it by doing research.

Research has some other important advantages, as well.

First, through research, you create something of your own, perhaps even something you can publish. You can submit your research to competitions, usually starting on a local level and working all the way up to the national level. Competitions look amazing on a résumé, and it's hard to join any competition without having a competitive product.

Second, by doing research, you meet motivated students who may be participating in activities you never dreamed existed. When you hear about something innovative from either a speaker or a competitor, you should write it down and follow up on it. There is *no* way that you or I or anyone else can know about every single opportunity in this vastly expanding world of education, so keep your ear to the ground. People who do research are cutting-edge, and you will become so, as well – guilty by association.

Third, you usually do research through an affiliation with a university or other large organization; you never know who you're going to meet. You may eventually conduct your own research investigation, like Janet did in the "Up Not Out" Chapter, but Janet started out working with professors at a university. By working with experts in a field, you may gain valuable letters of recommendation, as well as insight into universities that offer programs that wow you.

I think it's important at this point to talk about a few different programs, so you see the wide varieties of schools offering research opportunities.

The University of Arizona - Tucson, AZ
KEYS (Keep Engaging Youth in Science) Internships

The KEYS program at University of Arizona is geared toward students who want to eventually work in biological sciences. What's special about the program is that it doesn't specifically have students working on medical cases, but rather introduces students to the wide range of scientific disciplines involved in bioscience. The agreements you and your parents or guardians sign convey the intensity of this program; everyone needs to be on board.

- *Details*
    - Each participant will receive $800
    - It is a 6-week, competitive summer internship.
    - Students work alongside researchers in bioscience, biomedical science, or engineering

- o Students perform independent research in a working laboratory
- o Each student prepares an individual poster to present at the final poster session
- *Components of the Application*
  - o An application
  - o A personal statement of 500-700 words
    - Topic: Briefly describe your academic and life objectives. How will participating in the KEYS Research Internship help you to achieve those objectives and what personal strengths or attributes make you more competitive for the KEYS Research Internship? Please mention your specific interests in bioscience or biomedical research.
  - o Agreements from you and your parents or guardians
  - o Two recommendation letters
  - o Official transcripts
- Link
  http://www.pathwaystoscience.org/programhub.asp?sort=HSC-UArizona-KEYS

Louisiana State University Health Science Center - New Orleans, LA

As if living in New Orleans would not be fun enough, now you get to build your résumé in the process! Here's what's especially cool about this internship: it actually teaches you how to make a poster presentation. People always talk about research posters, but actually creating and presenting one seems pretty overwhelming to most of us mere mortals. Even if this program in particular isn't for you, you should ask other programs if they are as hands-on in guiding their students towards making meaningful presentations. A powerful presentation can earn you an award at a competition, which will bolster your application more than you know.

Summer Research Internship Program

- *Details*
  - The programs is coordinated by the medical branch of LSU
  - Participants receive a monthly pay of $1,300 during an 8-week research experience
  - Students perform research and prepare a poster for presentation

- o Students attend mandatory, weekly seminars
- o Students receive training on poster presentation and proper performance at scientific meetings
- *Components of the Application*
  - o A completed application form
  - o A cover letter describing your research interests and career goals
  - o A résumé that describes your education, research and/or work experience, and personal accomplishments
- Link

  http://www.medschool.lsuhsc.edu/genetics/summer_student_program.aspx

Baylor University - Waco, TX

So, not all junior researchers get paid, as you shall see. This Baylor program is high-quality, and the mentors do guide students in honing their presentation skills, which is really beneficial. Furthermore, it's only four weeks, so you don't have to commit your entire life to the research program. That's attractive, too. However, it comes with a hefty price tag. Financial aid is available for candidates who need assistance, but it's worth keeping in mind that you may not want to take out loans for this sort of program. There are many great opportunities that don't cost money. If you feel like this will tax your parents' bank accounts too much, keep looking.

High School Summer Science Research Program

- *Details*
  - Participants must pay for this program, roughly $2,500 – but some financial aid is available
  - Participants complete a four-week residential program on the Baylor campus
  - Students learn how to work with new research technology and methods
  - Students write their own abstracts and show their PowerPoint presentations on the last day of the program
- *Components of the Application*
  - A completed application online
  - A teacher recommendation
  - A character reference letter
  - An essay on your interest in science
  - A high school transcript
  - Your test scores – these might be reported on the transcript
- Link
  http://www.baylor.edu/summerscience/index.php?id=2346

Boston University - Boston, MA

This program is even more expensive than the Baylor program, but it's in Boston, perhaps the greatest college town in the United States, and it offers students an outstanding array of research choices. While some programs really focus on medicine and healthcare, the BU program lets participants find the field that interests *them*. So, if you want to study the physical limitations of a Sugar Glider's trajectory, BU will find a way for you to do it. It comes at a price, but if you can afford it or if you qualify for a scholarship, you should seriously consider it.

Boston University Research Internship in Science and Engineering Program

- *Details*
  - This 6-week honors program is available to rising seniors
  - Participants must pay for this program (about $5,000), but financial aid is available
  - Students may research in any field from psychology to medicine to mechanical engineering to astronomy
  - Students create a posters and present at a scientific conference at the end
- *Components of the Application*
  - A complete application online

- o A $50 nonrefundable application fee
- o An official transcript
- o A copy of your most recent ACT, SAT or PSAT scores
- o **One page,** single-spaced personal statement describing why you want to attend BU Research Internship in Science and Engineering. Also include what field you want to study and why
- o Two letters of recommendation, one from a science or math teacher and one from a guidance counselor
- Link
  http://www.bu.edu/summer/high-school-programs/research-internship/

The University of Texas MD Anderson Cancer Center - Smithville, TX

For those who haven't heard of MD Anderson, it is the leading cancer research center and hospital in the world. To have a chance to work with their unparalleled faculty and scientists would give any college application a huge boost, as well as provide you with an insight into the research that saves lives on a daily basis. This program is rigorous. It's long, and it's intense. You may not be able to travel all the way to Texas, but you should contact your local hospital to see if you can get involved in research there. Chances are, there's something out there for you.

High School Research Program

- *Details*
    - This program involves a paid internship – stipend not disclosed
    - Students complete a 10-week program, 40 hours per week
    - Students attend a weekly lecture series
    - Students present a 10-minute talk at the end to share their findings
    - The application is open to rising juniors and seniors
- *Components of the Application*
    - A completed application
    - An official transcript
    - 3 letters of recommendations from high school teachers
- Link:
    http://sciencepark.mdanderson.org/outreach/students/hs/

7

More than Money in the Bank

Meaningful Summer Work Experience

We've said it before, and we'll say it again: It's hard to make work look good on an application if you don't think long and hard about where you work. If you indicate on your application that you work to supplement family income, that's one thing, because it demonstrates that you had to get whatever job you could, just to help make ends meet at home. However, you look more committed to your community and future goals if you volunteer on the weekends, rather than working at the mall.

Most of us have parents who want us to work to learn the value of a dollar and to earn enough money to support our entertainment costs. That is definitely an important component of growing up, and it is a great thing to list on an application; however, some jobs look better than others, and work can't be your only activity.

We have helped kids in the past who have thrown themselves into their work, babysitting almost every night of the week and working on Saturdays and Sundays at retail jobs. Their work prevented them from doing anything else constructive, so they had no community service to list and no extracurricular activities. That's a bad thing. <u>There has to be balance on this application</u>, unless you were helping your mom and dad pay bills.

That said, we should discuss what you can do to maximize your work experience.

OPTION #1:
If possible, find jobs that mirror your interests.

Jobs at movie theaters and retail stores are fun, but they don't tell an admissions committee what you're all about. Unless, of course, you are applying for a film school or a merchandising program. And that's what we are talking about.

If you are interested in working in retail someday as a fashion merchandiser (someone who buys, sells, and/or promotes clothing), then working at Banana Republic might help you understand how fashion retailing works, and a job as a floor salesperson might benefit you when you move forward in your education. You need to indicate that on your application, and in your spare time, you should work on gaining as much knowledge as you can within the fashion retail industry.

Many college applications want a justification for why you have chosen a particular major. Furthermore, larger universities are often divided into smaller, more specific colleges, such as Business or the Arts. At that type of school, your chosen major will land you in one college at the university. Therefore, you are not actually competing against every other applicant to the university, but only those who have chosen that particular college. For example, the University of Texas at Austin has twelve undergraduate colleges (the McCombs School of Business, the Cockrell School of Engineering, the College of Communication, etc.).

Applicants to such universities must indicate their first and second-choice colleges, and they generally have an opportunity to explain their decisions. It's always better to have your work back up your choice. That gives you something to talk about in an optional essay, and if you have an interview, it helps you make a convincing case for your admission.

Suggested Jobs for Specific Majors

If you want to major in ….	You should consider a job or internship with ...
Political science	A local politician or political campaign
Marketing	An advertising agency or local magazine
Nursing	Doctor's office, as an office assistant or aide
Business	Any local company where you can see management in action
Film	Movie theater or production company, doing anything
Fashion	Art museum, boutique, or retail store
Natural science	Laboratory as an assistant, research assistant at a college – see summer research chapter
Hotel/Restaurant Management	Any restaurant, hotel, or tourist spot

Engineering	A construction or energy company
Architecture	Any design company... remember, you have to submit a portfolio!
Theater/Dance	As many local companies as possible —as many roles as possible. Keep track of all workshops!!
Social Work	Nonprofit organizations
Education	Babysitting, daycare, Sunday schools, etc.

OPTION #2:
Get Entrepreneurial!

As a high school student, your job opportunities may be limited. You can be smarter than the guy next to you, but you're just not old enough to be considered. Don't worry about it. The cool thing about being in high school is that as long as you're making an effort to do something different and good in the world, there's very little chance of your going wrong.

If you start a little company in your garage to earn some extra summer cash and get firsthand experience with the ups and downs of self-employment, what's the worst thing that could happen? It doesn't work out. Big deal!

No matter what comes of your business plan, you will have a new perspective on what it means to be in business in America. This is the land of free enterprise, but that doesn't mean that you can start a business without encountering a few pitfalls along the way. You might as well start encountering those obstacles while you're young!

Business ideas for budding young entrepreneurs:

- A lawn service
- A small tutoring operation
- A grocery delivery service
- A lunch delivery service to office buildings
- A day camp for kids
- An online venture – selling people's stuff on eBay, or starting your own site
- Making inexpensive jewelry and selling it at local boutiques
- A courier service
- An at-home car wash

What have we seen in action, and how have kids put their businesses together? Well, we've seen quite a few different ventures, each working out with varying degrees of success. We'll go through three different businesses that we've enjoyed watching grow, but these are by no means the only opportunities out there. You just need to sit down and ponder what you think you're capable of doing and what you think your neighborhood would accept and want.

Three Examples of Homegrown Student Businesses:

Business type	What did they do?	How did it go?
Car wash	- Knocked on neighbors' doors and offered to wash their cars - They charged about $20, which was less than the local detailing place	- Each girl walked away with roughly $2,000 cash per summer - They invested zero dollars in the company, so it was all profit
Day camp	- Offered a 5-day summer cooking camp for kids, ages 8-9 - Put fliers on neighbors' doors and let their Sunday Schools know about the camp - Charged $150 per camper - Taught kids how to make simple, safe snacks and meals	- Enrolling 6 kids per class, the girls walked away with $900 at the end of each week, $450 each - They kept costs low by making simple, kid-friendly food - The camp was a total hit, and they've continued the business through college

Jewelry-making	- Made bracelets out of leather strips - Made necklaces out of ribbons and old-school bottle caps - Made brooches out of fake flowers and rhinestone earrings	- These were the most financially successful ventures of all - Local boutiques love to pick up items made by people in the are - The people who made the jewelry used their creations to help them get into the top universities in the country, through the Arts Department

So, what if you want to "get entrepreneurial"?

What are some key points to keep in mind?

<u>Requirement #1</u>:

Don't do anything that requires a substantial investment of money on your part.

Beyond buying supplies for a carwash, paper to print fliers, or gas to deliver products, we don't recommend spending any real money. The most successful teen startup businesses are simple, done with easy-to-obtain materials. We realize that you may have lofty ambitions of founding a T-shirt business or a record label, but it costs money to buy the supplies involved in starting those businesses.

The less money you put into a business, the easier it is to get money out of it. Plus, it's easier to let go of a business that doesn't pan out if you don't feel like you have to break even.

Requirement #2:

Try to make the business something you can sustain for a few summers, or even through the school year.

Like every other activity we've suggested, with starting your small business, consistency is key. If you're getting to this at the last minute, no worries, make it the best you can in the time you have left in high school. But, if you're a freshman or a sophomore, try to put a little time towards this enterprise each summer. You can still do other things, but when you want to earn extra cash, you can turn to your business.

The longer you run an operation, the more you'll get to know about what works and what doesn't. You'll have more to talk about in an optional essay, so you can show what you would contribute to a particular college program.

Requirement #3:

Keep a good record of your business, so that you can track your profits and expenses.

Start a spreadsheet with a column labeled Expenses and a column labeled Income. Every time you buy something for business, put that number in the spreadsheet. Good records are the backbone of any successful operation, and you want to get in the habit of paying attention to the numbers from the start.

Furthermore, good records will allow you to make solid claims of success and experience in your application to college. You can explain what you've learned about managing finances and making smart business decisions.

Requirement #4:

Recruit your friends! Assign different tasks to people who would do them best.

Your friends are probably looking for something to do, too, so why not ask them to work with you on a summer work project?

Some people are going to be better at the creative end of a business, while others will be better at the detail-oriented, money matters. Figuring out how all of that works can really help you understand what it means to make a business tick.

You can delegate as follows:
  i.   Design and marketing –
        a. Making a logo
        b. Creating fliers and going out to post them
        c. Talking to organizations, like churches, about your new services
  ii. Money matters –
        a. Keeping track of receipts and recording all expenses
        b. Taking money from clients
        c. Holding onto cash and handling bank deposits or divvying up profits
  iii. Planning and operations –
        a. Determining which neighborhoods to target
        b. Coming up with the schedule

c. Making sure the work gets
done

This list could go on and on... these are just some ideas! Stay organized, divide responsibilities, and you'll have a great experience.

OPTION #3:
Internships

Internship is really the buzzword of the millennium. People talk about internships, but they really have no idea what they actually are. All they know is that someone's brother is doing one, and it's going to look really great on a college application.

Here's the reality:

An internship generally means a low-level job at a company where you can't get a real job without a serious application process. The goal of an internship is to learn about how a business works and get experience to put on a résumé. Many people are willing to do internships <u>for free</u>, so be prepared not to get paid.

Internships *do* look great on a college application, but they're pretty hard for a kid in high school to get. Your parents may know someone who owns a business, or they may help you get an internship at their own company.

Be aware, however, that you have to list your parent's employer on most applications, and admissions people are not stupid. They can easily put two-and-two together. This won't hurt you, but it makes your internship look less impressive.

The best internship programs are competitive. They're hard to get, and they're few and far between. So, you're going to have to <u>be resourceful</u>, **or** you're going to have to <u>pay a lot of money</u>.

Scenario #1: Being Resourceful
Going after something on your own

First, google high school internships in your city or state. You may find that you can do something at the mayor's office or at another part of city government that could be called an internship. Those internships tend to fly off the shelves, so if you don't get on this early, you may not get one. But, don't worry... You can find something if you take the initiative to do something different.

Second, start thinking about companies that have their locations around you. You may not be able to get a job at a doctor's office or law firm, but you *might* be able to get an internship. What's the difference? As an intern, you're basically volunteering for slave labor! Who doesn't love that?

It may sound excessive, but we think you should put together a list of 20 different businesses and get their phone numbers. Place a phone call to each business on the list to ask whether or not they would be interested in having a free intern to help with their chores over the summer.

Sample script:
Ring, Ring – receptionist answers...
Good morning, my name is _____.
Whom should I contact about getting an internship over the summer?

They transfer your call, either to a person or a voicemail...

My name is _____, and I am looking for an internship over the summer. I'd be willing to work for free to get an idea of how the business world works. Would it be possible for me to bring my résumé over to your office?

They may think this sounds weird, and they could ask you what type of job you'd like to do... You tell them you'd do any chores they asked. All you want is to get experience.

Some places will say 'no', but some places may actually say yes! You have absolutely no idea what will happen until you gut up and make the phone call.

Important note!

You need to make a résumé and take it over to the offices *in person*. Where will you make a résumé? There are plenty of online resources that will let you make one quickly. Don't spend money making a résumé for an internship. You can even do it through Microsoft Word's Resume Wizard.

Put any extracurricular activities you participate in, and list any leadership roles you've had. Also, don't forget to put the name of your high school and the month/year of your graduation. Don't stress about the paperwork you give them. You just want to show that you're dedicated.

Dedication is imperative!

Please note that it's tempting not to give 100% when you do a free internship; after all, you're not getting paid. That attitude won't win you any friends, however, and employers who detect your apathy won't stick their necks out for you when you're looking for a real job in the future.

However, if you put your heart and soul into your performance, you may secure an ongoing internship during college and build quality references for your eventual job search. No matter what, if you attempt to make the most of your internship, you will acquire valuable experience that will benefit you in any future work endeavor.

If you only want to ask for a two-week internship because you think you'll slack, then only sign up for two weeks!

Remember, your employer or internship coordinator can send in a supplemental letter of recommendation for you to colleges and scholarship committees.

Keys to Being an Impressive Intern

- Always say "Yes, Sir." and "Yes, Ma'am." Erase "yeah" from your vocabulary.
- Always arrive on time.
- Dress professionally – starched shirts, polished shoes, etc.
- Do even the silliest tasks with a smile.
- Write a letter of thanks at the end of your internship to show appreciation for the opportunity.

Scenario #2: Paying a Lot of Money
Guaranteed internship companies

These days, there are several companies that help high school students secure summer internships in big cities, like Boston, New York, and Los Angeles. Those companies do a great job, but they come with a hefty price tag – often upwards of $6,000 for a 4-week program.

If money is no object, then this may be an option for you, but if cash is tight <u>at all</u>, this is absolutely NOT worth the expense.

Internships add to your résumé, but they certainly will not get you into college. There is no reason to allocate your family's resources to such a costly program when, with some initiative, you can come up with something on your own.

We can't say it with enough vehemence: Do NOT spend money on an internship program unless your family has dollars lying around for you to fund summer activities! It won't pay off otherwise.

8

Studying Abroad

=

Cultural Awareness

We hesitated to write this section for a few reasons. First, study abroad programs can be synonymous for taking the lazy, party summer overseas. Second, many students pick the same programs in the same countries, so the *wow* factor diminishes. Third, study abroad programs are usually pricey, and we didn't want students to think they had to shell out a bunch of cash in order to look impressive on their applications.

Why, then, are we including this section in our new edition? Well, kids love studying abroad, and the experience provides a broader perspective of the world, preparing students to enter college with a multicultural approach. What you see on a study abroad trip – what you learn about yourself and others – can offer a basis for college admissions essays and augment your contributions in an interview setting. There is really no downside, but that still doesn't mean it's the right choice for everyone.

When you consider your study abroad options, you have to ask yourself several questions.

1. Which country should you choose?

First, you need to look at the stability of the country you're considering. Some countries are more stable than others, and that means they're less dangerous. Historically, people have been pretty safe in Western Europe and Japan, although there have been some scary natural disasters in Japan in recent years. Many students opt to study in Australia because it's gorgeous and extremely safe; others choose Argentina for its opposite climate, hoping to hit the slopes in July. If you want to read up on the safety and stability of the country, you should read what the United States government has to say: http://travel.state.gov/travel/travel_1744.html

In this chapter, <u>we'll only cover the countries we've personally visited</u> because we don't want to speak without firsthand knowledge. That said, most of the suggestions (although not all) will be European because their governments resemble our own and there's relatively easy access to most potential study abroad locations.

Second, you'll want to consider how common it is for students to study abroad in the country you're considering. *Lots* of kids study abroad in Spain, for example, and that sort of waters down the value of the experience in the eyes of admissions committees. That doesn't mean that you shouldn't study in Spain, but it does mean that you may want to consider an off-the-beaten path program there.

Third, you need to take your own travel experience into consideration. If you haven't traveled very much, then you may be nervous about going far from home. That's totally fine. In that case, look into the United Kingdom, Costa Rica, or Canada. All the countries in the United Kingdom speak English, so you won't be stressing out about a language barrier; Costa Rica and Canada are extremely close to the United States, so you won't have to leave the continent.

2. What does the program offer?

First, is it a camp or an educational opportunity? It's a lot harder to write about six weeks of kayaking and climbing in the Alps on a luxury camp than it is to write about the course, *Athens from Socrates to Hadrian* (obviously, the Alps might be more fun!). Both programs have their unique dynamics, but they're not equal. Got that? We would push you to do the academic program, of course, because it shows intellectual curiosity. If you really must do an outdoors program, then try to tack that on at the end.

Second, take a look at the course options. It might be interesting for you to take a class about the culture of the country you're visiting. Every program offers different courses, so don't just make a split-second decision. You never know what you'll find if you keep looking.

Finally, check into the living arrangements of the program. In some cases, you'll do a homestay, which means you'll be staying with a family; in others, you'll live in an apartment setting with your friends. If you are mainly going to improve your foreign language skills, do the homestay. You'll wind up having to communicate in the foreign language, whether you want to or not.

3. What are the dates of the program?

Is there any way you could do this program AND something else? Perhaps you can do this and a community service project. You should take a look at your summer overall and see where the dates line up. That way, you'll be able to schedule multiple activities without running into a snag. In many cases, it's better to pick something that starts early or late in the summer, so you can split your summer in half. Look into this early and think ahead.

4. Does the program have any requirements?

Language-based abroad programs may require that you have a certain number of language credits to attend. You don't want to get your heart set on a program only to find out that you don't meet their specifications.

Other programs have behavior requirements, and this may be critical to some of you. The reality is, these programs have liability concerns, which means they can't afford for you to get hurt while you're their responsibility. They can't have you getting drunk and falling down the stairs or getting mugged at a nightclub in the wee hours of the morning. What does this mean to you? You may have to use a breathalyzer, and if you're caught drinking, you'll be sent home. In other cases, you'll have to conform to some strict curfew rules, and you may not get much time to yourself. Seriously, this doesn't matter. You're going to experience a culture, and if you're living with a host family, you'll get the immersion that will build your ability to interact with the world. Don't let these limitations on your freedom prevent you from participating in a study abroad program; just suck it up for three weeks. If you go, you can have a wonderful time, and most of our students do. You just have to abide by the rules.

Country #1: Spain

This may be the most popular study abroad country. Many students focus on Spanish in school, and when they think of a place that sounds fun and different, Spain usually pops up on the radar. I feel especially comfortable talking about Spain: it's where I studied abroad, and I have spent many vacations there since that time.

Spain has a different feel from other European countries. It's modern, but it still holds onto the low-key ways of the past. Depending upon where you study, you'll get different vibes from the Spanish people. In Madrid, Barcelona, and Bilbao, they're hardworking and fast-moving, and the siesta is a thing of the past; in Alicante, Sevilla, and Granada, the pace is slower, and businesses really shut down in the afternoon to allow people to take their much-needed naps, especially during summer. However, no matter which city you choose, you will find yourself immersed in a culture that loves a good time, appreciates beauty, and feels fierce national pride.

If you're investigating study abroad in Spain, make sure your programs allow you to go out to eat at normal Spanish hours. I worked in Sevilla on a study abroad program, and the students had to eat at 7:00 P.M. because the program wanted to keep them on an American schedule. Since food is such an enormous part of life in Spain, that arrangement was a serious letdown for the kids on the trip. However, they were staying in a hotel and were, therefore, bound to the group at all times. That's one reason I support the homestay experience so sincerely: you get to live the lifestyle like a native.

Country #2: France

France is also incredibly popular with students. As a country, France may have the greatest cultural mystique: it just emanates character, beauty, and lust for life. In movies, France gets a pretty bad rap. The French are portrayed as rude and unaccommodating for the most part, but you have to remember that the media likes to overplay *everything*. Are people rude in France? In my experience, No. Of course, people in Paris might be a little snooty, but big cities are always that way! You just have to get out into the countryside of France; don't kid yourself into thinking that Paris is France. Paris is a beautiful city in France, but there is so much more.

We recommend going south in France to Aix-en-Provence or the French Riviera because they're beautiful and have the mountains, the beach, and gorgeous countryside. Your only possible concern is that you might wind up staying in the country, but for a true immersion experience, this might be the best possible situation. What's the point of living in a French city that has all the same trappings of an American city? Small towns in France have their own special allure – amazing bakeries, small fishmonger stores, incredible butcher shops – and you will see a slice of life that has never really existed in the United States. We definitely recommend a homestay in southern France because you need to witness the real way of life in a countryside that has only embraced modern times on its own terms.

While we think Provence and the French Riviera are perhaps the most charming regions in France, that doesn't mean that you shouldn't consider other destinations, as well. It's merely a suggestion. You could consider Orleans, Toulouse, or Montpellier. All are terrific summer destinations where you can blend into French culture for a magnificent two-to-four weeks. What we don't want you to do, however, is get locked into a program in Paris, unless you know the city and are certain that's where you want to spend a substantial amount of time. The likelihood is that any program you take to France will start and end in Paris, so you'll get to go to the Eiffel Tower, the Notre Dame Cathedral, and the Louvre. You just may not want to spend all of your time there.

Country #3: Italy

Who can say enough about Italy? It may be the most beautiful country in the world. It's one of the few countries that I would recommend without reservation, no matter which region you choose to visit. From Turin in the north to Messina in the south, Italy's countryside varies in its topography and vegetation, but it never strays from deserving the adjective gorgeous. The cultural history here is so rich that everywhere you turn, you see evidence of its majesty, and the people have a forcefulness of national character that I've never witnessed anywhere else. Even if you spent the entire summer in Italy, it would not be enough.

So, where do I recommend that you study? Many students choose to go to Florence because it's small and manageable, and, due to its role in the Renaissance, it's one of the world's most important cities. Florence is right in the middle of Tuscany, so there are multiple cultural excursions you can take into the countryside. Plus, it's an easy train ride to most other larger cities in Italy. Finally, Florence is also the city with the greatest abundance of high school study abroad options. Therefore, if you choose Italy for study abroad, this is probably where you'll end up.

Italy may be a good destination for you if language is not your forte. That's because most Italian programs do not require a language prerequisite. In France or Spain, it may be expected that you have a cursory understanding of the language, but Italian study abroad programs understand that Italian does not show up as an optional foreign language at most American high schools. That means that you'll probably take only cultural classes, given in English, and any language class you might take would be extremely basic. Additionally, you'll probably live in a dorm in Italy because practicing the language may not be as important to you as it would be in France or Spain.

Country #4: Greece

Greece is like nothing else, and we wouldn't recommend studying there to the fainthearted. As a matter of fact, you won't find many programs that will take you there because in recent years, Greece has acquired a reputation of instability. It's true that Greece has its political and economic issues, but it is still an extremely interesting destination, where you can get lost in a world of history and caught up in a culture of enthusiasm and passion.

While we love Athens, we wouldn't necessarily recommend studying there. In fact, most programs will only take you through Athens briefly. Others will have you study in Thessaloniki, a less volatile city than Athens in northern Greece. Thessaloniki is vibrant – filled with delicious food and fantastic music, close to both the beaches and the mountains. Many say it is the most progressive city in Greece.

In Greece, you'll take courses on Western Civilization and Greek culture. You may take an elementary Modern Greek course, but you probably won't have to. Many people in Greece speak English, so learning the language – while always culturally important – won't be a necessity. Additionally, you might find that you can do a combined Greece-Italy trip, which may be the best option. You'll probably get to see some islands and hit the hot spots in both countries.

Country #5: England

England is a wonderful place to spend the summer, especially June. It's about the only time that the clouds let up for long periods at a time, and you'll be surprised how green and charming the countryside looks in that yellow summer sun. We recommend England overall.

London is an excellent city with wonderful public transportation and incredible variety. It's just terribly expensive. Let me repeat that: It's *terribly* expensive. In England, the currency is the Pound, and it just carries tremendous value. Buying anything in London costs about double what it does in the United States, and you should keep that in mind if you're going to study there. The fact is, most Americans are unprepared for the exchange rate, and the strength of the pound can destroy even the most generous American budget. However, most study abroad programs factor that extra cost into their price, and if you mainly eat with the group and don't shop too much, you'll do fine.

You'll find an abundance of study abroad options in England, and my favorite is probably the opportunity to study at Oxford University through Oxford Advanced Studies Program. But, don't kid yourself, this is a real study program, and you'll be accepted on the basis of your grades and letters of recommendation. Still, what could possibly look better on a college application than a summer at Oxford, especially if you get the chance to explain the work you completed during that time? To read more about this specific program, go to:

http://www.oasp.ac.uk/summerprogram/

Country #6: Germany

Germany is definitely best visited for the first time during the summer. The winters can be bitterly cold, but the summers are bright green. The German people are friendly, and almost everyone speaks English, probably more properly than your friends at home.

If I were going to study in Germany, I would make sure that the trip involved some time in Berlin. It's such an exciting city, and it just feels young. That youthful air in Berlin exists because the city is still in the process of rebuilding after decades behind the Iron Curtain of the Cold War. You will see stretches of the Berlin Wall and walk by the historic Brandenburg Gate, and you will be surprised by the vibrancy of East Berlin, where the revival is in its fullest form. Berlin has very manageable public transportation, so you will be able to get around with ease. It doesn't matter where in the city you stay; you'll have access to all parts of Berlin.

You may be able to take a side trip from Berlin to Prague because it's only a short train ride (4 hours), and the chances are, your program will already include the excursion. Everyone loves Prague because it's magically well-preserved. It's really a must-see if you're anywhere nearby, so try to schedule a visit.

Country #7: Thailand

Thailand is cropping up more and more on people's agendas, and for good reason. Thailand has a stable monarchy and a relatively wealthy economy. Bangkok is extremely sophisticated, with shopping malls and cultural opportunities that can match those of any city in the world. Most people – although definitely not all – speak a modest amount of English. Thailand is far away, though, even farther than you think, because it is truly nothing like home.

Most study abroad trips to Thailand involve studying ecological and environmental issues. Other programs involve community service in orphanages or in rice fields or with elephants, and all of those opportunities have the potential to provide great personal rewards to you as a traveler. However, the living conditions will probably be far from glamorous on ANY of those programs. While the chance to live in the Thai countryside might seem like the perfect rustic opportunity for the rugged adventurer, for some of us, it's just too risky. That's perfectly fine! We just wanted to include Thailand because it is safe, beautiful, and special; however, if you're anti-roughing it, then Thailand may not be the destination for you. Still, you should Google the beaches in Phuket and the temples in Chiang Mai, just to see how diverse and incredible the country is.

Study Abroad Opportunities

Note: Although we're picking one program to explore in each of the countries we've mentioned, almost all of the companies discussed in this section offer trips to multiple destinations, so go browse their websites. There will be programs to all sorts of different countries, many of which we didn't discuss earlier in the chapter because we wanted to focus only on the places we knew well. You just need to do your own research about each possible location and figure out which opportunity suits your needs.

1. Bridges Study Abroad Program, Focus on **Spain**

Where? The legendary resort city of San Sebastián, Spain

What? Language course

When? A variety of dates, ranging from 2 – 4 weeks

Housing? Homestay

Requirements? 2 years of Spanish, 14-18 years of age with a 2.5 GPA.

How much? Prices start at $4,200

Link to check it out:
http://www.bridgesstudyabroad.com/sebastian.htm

2. Edu-Culture Dorm and Homestay Program, Focus on **France**

   Where? Aix-en-Provence, France

   What? Combination of language classes in Aix-en-Provence and immersion experience in the small town of Hyeres along the coast.

   When? June 28 – July 25

   Housing? Dorm in Aix-en-Provence; Homestay in Hyeres

   Requirements? 2 years of high school French. Must be 14-18 years of age.

   How much? $6,995

Link to check it out:
http://educulture.org/programs/france/aix-en-provence/

3. Abbey Road Programs, Focus on **Italy**
   Where? Florence, Italy
   What? Cultural and language courses in Florence – ranging from Fashion Design to Soccer to Art History
   When? June 28 – July 26
   Housing? Apartments with residential advisors
   Requirements? None
   How much? $7,795, *scholarships available*
   Link to check it out:
   http://www.goabbeyroad.com/summer-programs/italy/florence.shtml

4. Greek Summer, Focus on **Greece**
   Where? Based out of Thessaloniki, but most time is spent in a farming community in rural Greece.
   What? Service and adventure project. Learn about agriculture AND climb Mt. Olympus.
   When? June 24 – July 31
   Housing? With host family
   Requirements? Enthusiasm and dedication.

How much? $6,000
Link to check it out:
http://www.greeksummer.org/page/default.
asp?la=2&id=114

5. Oxbridge Academic Programs, Focus on
   England
   Where? Cambridge, England
   What? The Cambridge Tradition program,
   offering a wide variety of courses on the
   Cambridge University campus
   When? July 8 – August 4
   Housing? University dormitories
   Requirements? No language requirement.
   Must be entering 10th – 12th grades in the fall.
   How much? $7,595
   Link to check it out:
   http://www.oxbridgeprograms.com/the-
   cambridge-tradition/

6. Ayusa Summer Cultural Exploration, Focus on
   Germany
   Where? Berlin, Germany
   What? Summer language immersion in Berlin
   with an excursion to Prague
   When? July – August (4 weeks)
   Housing? Homestay

Requirements? No language requirement. Must be 16-18 years of age with a 2.5 GPA.
How much? $6,295
Link to check it out:
http://www.ayusa.org/students/study-abroad/germany/summer

7. Lifeworks International, focus on **Thailand**
Where? Bangkok, Thailand
What? Service learning expedition to work with children in two rural villages, as well as adventure experiences throughout the Thai countryside.
When? July 20 – August 9
Housing? Hotel stay in Bangkok, dormitory housing in rural provinces
How much? $4,870
Link to check it out: http://www.lifeworks-international.com/thailand/overview.php

Please note that we *know* the options listed above are extremely pricey. There are definitely less expensive options out there, but we don't feel good about endorsing any program that we don't feel is 100% safe and reputable. We work with kids, and this book is geared towards improving students' chances of getting accepted to college. We really can't afford to put anyone at risk. However, you can do your own research and find programs that suit your needs/budget.

If you decide to go out and find your own summer study abroad opportunity, just make sure you do plenty of research. Call the companies that pop up on the internet and talk to the representatives. Don't be shy. Ask plenty of questions. Remember, these study abroad companies *want* you to pick their program, so you're in charge.

Finally, if you fall desperately in love with a program that's out of your price range, try to think outside the box to find funding. Talk to your religious and community organizations about raising money to help you fund the trip. Also, there are scholarships that can help you pay for summer programs. Usually, the programs themselves will have a limited number of available scholarships, and those are probably your best bet. However, private organizations also offer scholarships for study abroad experiences, but they're few in number and hard to find. You'll have to do some serious searching. – If you manage to put the money together, don't forget to put that on your résumé! It shows serious commitment, ingenuity, and spunk. Colleges will love seeing those qualities in action.

9

So What? Now What?

Wrapping it up

Thus far, we've given you information about the myriad summer programs that exist and walked you through examples to highlight the many opportunities that are eagerly waiting for you to find them. However, we realize that all this material can be a little overwhelming if you don't really understand what to do with it. What should you do now?

You need to begin by mapping out what you're going to do this summer. Refer back to the list of activities you created for Chapter 1, and see where your gaps lie. Do you need community service hours? Can you sign up NOW for the President's Volunteer Service Award, to start tracking your hours today?

With all the knowledge you've gained about the possibilities for summer résumé improvement, you are well on your way towards becoming a competitive college applicant. Remember, while the résumé comprises only one component of the college application, its contents can convey to admissions committees your personality, interests, and commitment.

If you want more information about specific programs, please check out:
www.allinoneacademics.com.

We strive to keep the All-in-One Academics website as current as possible about free resources and admissions information. You can check out our blog if you want to read breaking college news, or post comments on our forums to be moderated by our staff.

No matter what you do, stay active in this process, so you'll always be ahead of the pack. Your friends may be baffled by what you're doing, but in the end, they'll wish they had jumped on your bandwagon.

We hope this book has been helpful in getting you started on the road to an enviable college résumé. Be sure to check out our college applications courses and online support when it's time for you to actually apply to college. We are committed to assisting you in achieving the educational goals you've already set and the ones you haven't even dreamed of yet.

All-in-One Academics
Online Resources:
www.allinoneacademics.com

The Résumé Builder:

When you start filling up your calendar and creating a record of success, you're going to need to keep track of it all. Our online Résumé Builder allows you to create your own account, where you can store information about your extracurricular activities, community service, internship experience, etc.

And, whenever you're ready to create a résumé, whether it's for college applications or internship purposes, your information can be immediately transformed into a perfectly formatted word document or PDF for download. There is truly no other résumé service as thorough and targeted for students as our Résumé Builder. After you've put in so much effort to enhance and demonstrate your potential, you owe to yourself to present your experiences well on paper.

Common Application Supplement Topics:

This information may not be useful to you until your senior year, but you will certainly need it then! We keep a running list of all supplemental essay topics, so you don't have to log in and out of your Common Application account every time you're interested in researching a school's requirements.

College Admissions Blog:

We are constantly watching the college admissions process. Constantly. And, we report about what we hear and see in the news and in our students' results. This is an evolving document that chronicles the changes in the system and helps you make educated choices about your future.

You will also find some unique college reviews on our blog. We take trips regularly to different schools around the country of all shapes and sizes. As usual, we take a different approach to college reviews, trying to cut through the obvious marketing to determine what kinds of students would be happy where.

No matter what, remember that **we are here** to help you be the best you can be. Check with our experts any time you need advice or ideas. You are on the road to greatness, and we can't wait to see what happens next!